Quick Gifts from the Kitchen
No Cooking Required

Gloria Hander Lyons

Blue Sage Press

D1522016

Quick Gifts from the Kitchen
No Cooking Required

Inquires should be addressed to:
Blue Sage Press
48 Borondo Pines
La Marque, TX 77568
www.BlueSagePress.com

ISBN: 978-0-9802244-6-7

Library of Congress Control Number: 2008911522

First Edition: December 2008

Printed in the United States of America

Table of Contents

Introduction

Quick Gifts from the Kitchen

In today's hectic, commercially driven world, making your own gifts is a way to return to a simpler time when most gifts were homemade treasures. Not only are handmade gifts unique, they are also easier on your gift-giving budget than the mass-produced items found in stores.

This book includes more than fifty mix recipes that you can stir up in a jiffy—no cooking required—to make inexpensive, one-of-a-kind gifts that your family and friends will enjoy.

With tasty recipes like Orange Spice Cappuccino Mix, Cranberry Cornbread Muffin Mix, Chicken Tortilla Soup Mix and Chocolate-Cinnamon Popcorn Spice, you'll find something for everyone on your list.

Also included is a helpful, step-by-step guide for assembling beautiful gift baskets, plus instructions for making fabric gift bags and decorating paper gift sacks to hold your mixes, creative ideas for packaging, and gift tags to photocopy and cut out.

Making your own gifts is not only rewarding for yourself, but a special treat for your lucky recipient. You'll feel a sense of accomplishment and pride, while the person receiving the gift will feel honored that you used your time and talent to create a "one-of-a-kind" gift just for them.

Whether you need a last minute gift for a co-worker or a carload of inexpensive gifts for those on your Christmas list, you'll never need to be stressed over giving again. You'll have the perfect solution to solve those pesky gift-giving dilemmas.

These mix recipes are not only fun, quick and easy to make, they are proven crowd pleasers. When you're puzzled about what to give to someone you don't know well or someone who seems to have everything, food is always a good choice.

Quick Gifts from the Kitchen will help make your gift-giving a joyful experience. Instead of wasting time on futile shopping trips and over-spending on mass produced store-bought items, create your own special gifts from the heart.

Everyone on your gift list will be glad you did!

Hot Beverage Mixes

Forget-Me-Not Tea Mix

1 (15 oz.) jar instant orange
breakfast drink mix
1 cup granulated sugar
1 cup unsweetened instant tea
powder
1/2 cup presweetened lemonade mix
 1 (0.14 oz.) package unsweetened cherry-flavored soft
    drink mix
2 teaspoons ground cinnamon
1 teaspoon ground nutmeg

In a large bowl, combine all ingredients until well blended.
Recipe makes about 4 cups of tea mix. Place 2 cups of mix
in a one-pint canning jar and decorate lid with a fabric
circle (instructions on page 59). Or place 2 cups of mix in a
plastic zipper-type bag. Place plastic bag inside a fabric bag
(instructions on page 56). Tie closed with ribbon, jute or
raffia tied into a bow. Attach cooking instruction tag.

Gift basket idea: Place fabric bag of mix in a basket with a
mug and a mug mat.

Forget-Me-Not Tea Mix

To Serve: Place 2 heaping
tablespoons of mix into a
mug. Add 8 ounces of hot
water. Stir until blended.

3

Chai Tea Latte Mix

1/4 cup granulated sugar
2 tablespoons instant nonfat dry milk
2 tablespoons powdered coffee creamer
2 tablespoons powdered French vanilla coffee creamer
2 tablespoons unsweetened instant tea
1/4 teaspoon ground cinnamon
1/4 teaspoon ground ginger
1/16 teaspoon ground cloves

Blend all ingredients and process in blender or food processor until mixture is a fine powder. Recipe makes about 3/4 cup of mix (about 4 servings). Place mix in a decorative tin or canister with an airtight lid. Or place in a plastic zipper-type bag. Place plastic bag inside a fabric bag (instructions on page 56). Tie closed with ribbon, jute or raffia tied into a bow. Attach cooking instruction tag.

Gift basket idea: Place fabric bag of mix in a basket with a mug and a mug mat.

Party favor idea: Place 1 serving (3 tablespoons) mix in a tiny zipper-type plastic bag or bundle in a double layer of plastic wrap. Place in bowl of a heavy-duty plastic teaspoon. Wrap a 6" square of fabric around the mix and gather around the neck of the spoon. Tie with raffia or ribbon. Attach cooking instruction tag to ribbon.

Chai Tea Latte Mix

To Serve: Place 3 tablespoons of mix into a mug. Add 1 cup of boiling water. Stir until blended.

Herbal Tea Blend

3/4 cup loose black tea leaves
1/4 cup dried sage leaves, crumbled
3 tablespoons dried thyme leaves
1 tablespoon dried, grated lemon peel

Combine ingredients in a small bowl until well blended. Recipe makes 1-1/4 cups of tea blend. Place mix in a small plastic zipper-type bag and place bag and cooking instructions inside a small tin canister or decorative Chinese take-out container.

Gift basket idea: Place the tin of tea blend in a basket along with a pretty cup and saucer, a tea ball or tea strainer and a jar of flavored honey. You can also add a fabric gift bag of scone mix (page 15).

Herbal Tea Blend

To Serve: Place 2 teaspoons tea blend in a warmed teapot for every 8 ounces of hot water used. Pour boiling water over tea and steep 3-5 minutes. Strain into cups and serve with lemon slices and honey.

Hazelnut Mocha Mix

1 (1 lb., 9.6 oz.) package instant nonfat dry milk powder
1 (16 oz.) package powdered sugar, sifted
1 (15 oz.) package chocolate mix for milk
1 (11 oz.) jar non-dairy powdered coffee creamer
2 (8 oz.) jars hazelnut-flavored non-dairy powdered coffee
 creamer
1/2 cup cocoa powder
1/4 cup instant coffee granules

In a very large bowl, combine all ingredients. Recipe makes about 18 cups of mix. Place 2 cups of mix into a one-pint wide-mouth canning jar. Decorate jar with fabric circle as described on page 59. Or place 2 cups mix in a plastic zipper-type bag. Place plastic bag inside a fabric bag (instructions on page 56). Close with jute or raffia tied into a bow. Attach cooking instruction tag.

For a gift basket idea: Place fabric bag of mix in a basket with a mug and a fabric gift bag of muffin mix (page 17).

Hazelnut Mocha Mix

To Serve: Place 3 tablespoons mix into a mug. Add 6 ounces of hot water. Stir until well blended.

Orange Spice Cappuccino Mix

1/2 cup non-dairy powdered coffee
  creamer
1/2 cup granulated sugar
1/4 cup instant coffee granules
2 teaspoons dried, ground orange
  peel
1 teaspoon ground cinnamon

In a small bowl, combine all ingredients until well blended. Recipe makes about 2-1/4 cups of mix. Divide mix evenly into two separate small zipper-type plastic bags.

Place each bag in the center of a 14" square of homespun or print fabric, or use a fabric napkin. Gather the fabric around the mix and tie with ribbon, jute or raffia. Attach cooking instruction tag. Place mix inside a mug. Or place mix in a decorative tin or canister with an airtight lid.

For a gift basket idea: Place the mug and the fabric bundle of drink mix inside a basket along with a fabric gift bag filled with scone mix (page 15).

Orange Spice
Cappuccino Mix

To Serve: Place 2 teaspoons mix into a mug. Add 2/3 cup of boiling water. Stir until well blended.

Malted Cocoa Mix

1 (25.6 oz.) package instant nonfat dry milk
6 cups miniature marshmallows
1 (16 oz.) container instant cocoa mix for milk
1 (13 oz.) jar malted milk powder
1 cup sifted powdered sugar
1 (6 oz.) jar non-dairy powdered coffee creamer
1/2 teaspoon salt

In a very large bowl, combine all ingredients until well blended. Recipe makes about 20 cups of mix. Place 2 cups of mix into a one-pint wide-mouth canning jar. Decorate jar with fabric circle as described on page 59 and attach cooking instruction tag. Or place 2 cups mix in a plastic zipper-type bag. Place plastic bag inside a fabric gift bag (see instructions on page 56). Close with ribbon, jute or raffia tied into a bow. Attach cooking instruction tag.

For a gift basket idea: Place fabric gift bag of mix in a basket with a mug and a bag of cookie mix (page 21).

Malted Cocoa Mix

To Serve: Place 1/3 cup of mix into a mug. Add 6 ounces of hot water. Stir until well blended.

Mint Hot Chocolate Mix

1-1/4 cups instant non-fat dry milk
1/4 cup instant hot cocoa mix for milk
1/4 cup mint chocolate chips
2 tablespoons non-dairy powdered coffee creamer
1 teaspoon ground cinnamon

In a small bowl, combine all ingredients until well blended. Recipe makes about 2 cups of mix. Place mix in a one-pint wide-mouth canning jar. Decorate jar with fabric circle as described on page 59 and attach cooking instruction tag. Or place mix in a plastic zipper-type bag. Place plastic bag inside a fabric gift bag (see instructions on page 56). Close with ribbon, jute or raffia tied into a bow. Attach cooking instruction tag.

For a gift basket idea: Place fabric bag of mix in a basket with a mug and a bag of cookie mix (page 21).

Mint Hot Chocolate Mix

To Serve: Place 1/3 cup of mix into a mug. Add 1 cup of boiling water. Stir until chocolate chips are melted.

Snowman Soup Mix

1 cup instant nonfat dry milk
2/3 cup white chocolate baking
   chips
3 tablespoons vanilla flavor
   powdered coffee creamer

Combine all ingredients in a food processor or blender and process until finely ground. Recipe makes about 1-1/2 cups mix (about 4 servings).

Place mix in a decorative tin or canister with an airtight lid. Or place in a plastic zipper-type bag. Place plastic bag inside a fabric bag (instructions on page 56). Tie closed with ribbon, jute or raffia tied into a bow. Attach cooking instruction tag.

Gift basket idea: Place fabric bag of mix in a basket with a mug and a mug mat.

Individual Gift Idea: Place 1/3 cup mix (1 serving) in a plastic zipper-type bag. Place the bag in a cellophane bag. Tie the top closed with ribbon and attach instruction tag. Place cellophane bag inside a mug.

Snowman Soup Mix

To Serve: Place 1/3 cup mix into a mug. Add 1 cup of boiling water. Stir until well blended.

Apple Cider Mull Mix

For each mull mix bundle, you will need:
2 (8") squares of cheesecloth
White string for tying bundles closed

Ingredients:
2 tablespoons loose leaf black tea
4 teaspoons whole cloves
1 tablespoon whole allspice
2 cinnamon sticks, broken into large pieces
1 teaspoon dried orange peel

In a small bowl, blend all ingredients together. Place in center of cheesecloth squares. Bring corners of cheesecloth together and tie closed with string. Place in a small plastic zipper-type bag. Place plastic bag inside a fabric bag (instructions on page 56). Tie closed with jute or raffia tied into a bow. Attach a cinnamon stick and cooking instructions to the bow.

Or place mix bundle in a plastic bag, then place inside a colorful Chinese take-out container found at craft stores. Add an artificial spring of greenery to the top.

Apple Cider Mull Mix

To Prepare: Combine 1 gallon of apple cider with 1/2 cup granulated sugar in a large Dutch oven. Add cheesecloth bag of mull mix and bring to a boil over medium heat. Cover and simmer for 20 minutes. Discard mull mix. Serve hot. Makes 16 cups of mulled apple cider.

Spiced Wine Mix

3/4 cup brown sugar, firmly packed
2 teaspoons ground cinnamon
1 teaspoon ground cloves
1/2 teaspoon dried, grated lemon peel
1/2 teaspoon dried, grated orange peel
1 teaspoon ground allspice
1/2 teaspoon ground nutmeg

In a small bowl, combine all ingredients until well blended. Recipe makes about 3/4 cup of mix (4 servings).

Place mix in a plastic zipper-type bag. Place plastic bag inside a fabric gift bag made from velvet or brocade fabric (see page 56 for instructions) and tie closed with ribbon or a tassel. Attach cooking instructions and a cinnamon stick.

To give as a gift basket, place fabric bag of mix in a basket along with a bottle of red wine and one or two clear glass mugs.

Spiced Wine Mix

To Prepare: Combine 1/4 cup of mix with 1 cup red wine and 1/4 cup of water in a small saucepan. Bring to a boil over medium heat; reduced heat and simmer 5 minutes. Makes 1 serving.

Breakfast Treats

Almond Pancake Mix

3 cups instant nonfat dry milk
2-1/2 cups all-purpose flour
1 cup whole-wheat flour
1 cup finely ground almonds
2/3 cup baking powder
1/3 cup granulated sugar
1 tablespoon salt

In a large bowl, combine all ingredients until well blended. Recipe makes about 7-1/2 cups of mix. Place 2-1/2 cups of mix into 3 separate plastic zipper-type bags. Place each bag of mix into a fabric gift bag (see page 56 for instructions) and tie closed with ribbon, jute or raffia. Tie on a spatula with the bow.

To give as a gift basket, place mix inside a basket along with a bottle of maple syrup. Or place in a small skillet or griddle. Attach the cooking instruction tag.

Almond Pancake Mix

To Prepare: In a medium bowl, combine pancake mix, 1-1/4 cups water, 1 egg and 2 tablespoons vegetable oil. Stir just until moistened. Heat a greased griddle over medium heat. For each pancake, pour about 1/4 cup batter onto griddle and cook until top is full of bubbles. Turn with a spatula and cook until remaining side is golden brown. Re-grease griddle as needed. Serve with butter and syrup. Makes about 1 dozen 5" pancakes.

Gingerbread Pancake Mix

1-1/2 cups whole wheat flour
1/2 cup all-purpose flour
6 tablespoons brown sugar, packed
2 teaspoons baking powder
1 teaspoon ground ginger
1/2 teaspoon ground cinnamon
1/2 teaspoon salt
1/4 teaspoon ground cloves
4 teaspoons instant coffee granules (package separately)

In a large bowl, combine all ingredients except coffee granules. Recipe makes about 2 cups of mix. Place in a plastic zipper-type bag. Bundle coffee granules in a double layer of plastic wrap or place in a tiny plastic bag. Place mix and coffee granules inside a fabric gift bag (see instructions on page 56). Tie top closed with jute and attach a spatula and cooking instruction tag.

Gift basket idea: Include fabric bag of mix in a basket or skillet filled with colorful paper shred, along with a couple of jars of fruit flavored syrup.

Gingerbread Pancake Mix

To Prepare: Place coffee granules in 1/2 cup boiling water; stir until dissolved and cool completely. In a medium bowl, blend together 1-1/3 cups milk, 2 eggs, 2 tablespoons vegetable oil and coffee. Add pancake mix and stir just until moistened. Cook 1/4 cup of batter on a greased griddle until bubbles form on top. Flip and cook other side until golden brown. Makes sixteen 4" pancakes.

Peach Nutmeg Scone Mix

2-1/2 cups biscuit baking mix
1/4 cup brown sugar, packed
1/4 cup granulated sugar
1/2 teaspoon ground nutmeg
3/4 cup dried peaches, chopped
1/2 cup almonds, chopped

In a large bowl, combine all ingredients until well blended. Recipe makes about 4-1/4 cups of mix. Place mix in a plastic zipper-type bag. Place plastic bag inside a fabric gift bag (see page 56 for instructions) and tie closed with ribbon, raffia or jute. Or place in a paper gift bag (see page 57 for ideas). Attach a biscuit cutter and cooking instruction tag to bow.

For a gift basket idea: Place fabric bag of mix inside a mixing bowl filled with paper shred, along with an oven mitt and a bottle of almond extract.

Peach Nutmeg Scone Mix

To Prepare: Preheat oven to 400°. Empty mix into a large bowl. In a separate bowl, blend 1 large egg, 1 teaspoon vanilla or almond extract and 1/3 cup milk. Add egg mixture to scone mix and stir just until moistened. Turn dough out onto a lightly floured surface and knead gently 10-12 strokes or until smooth. Pat dough to 3/4" thickness. Cut out scones using a 2-1/2" to 3" biscuit cutter and place 1" apart on a lightly greased baking sheet. Brush tops with milk and sprinkle with sugar. Bake 15-18 minutes or until done. Serve warm with butter. Makes 8-9 scones.

Christmas Scone Mix in a Jar or Bag

2-1/2 cups biscuit baking mix
1/4 cup brown sugar, gently packed
1/4 cup granulated sugar
1 teaspoon dried grated orange peel
1 teaspoon ground cinnamon
3/4 cup dried cranberries, chopped
1/2 cup pecans, chopped

Pour baking mix into a 1-quart wide-mouth canning jar. Tap gently on a lightly padded surface on the counter to settle. Sprinkle brown sugar over baking mix and press down to pack. Mix granulated sugar with orange peel and cinnamon and pour over the brown sugar. Tap jar gently to settle. Add cranberry pieces then pecans and press down gently. Decorate jar with fabric circle as described on page 59 and attach cooking instruction tag and a 3" star-shaped cookie cutter. –OR– Mix all ingredients together and place in a plastic bag. Place bag of mix in a paper gift sack (see decorating directions on page 57).

Christmas Scone Mix

To Prepare: Preheat oven to 400°. Empty mix into a large bowl and stir. In a separate bowl, blend 1 large egg and 1/3 cup sour cream. Add egg mixture to scone mix and stir just until moistened. Turn dough out onto a lightly floured surface and knead gently until smooth. Pat dough to 3/4" thickness. Cut out scones using a 2-1/2" to 3" biscuit cutter or star-shaped cookie cutter and place 1" apart on a lightly greased baking sheet. Brush tops with milk and sprinkle with sugar. Bake 15-18 minutes or until done. Serve warm with butter. Makes 8-9 scones.

Apple Walnut Muffin Mix

2 cups self-rising flour
1/2 cup granulated sugar
1/4 cup brown sugar, packed
2 teaspoons ground cinnamon
1/4 teaspoon ground nutmeg
1/2 cup chopped walnuts
1 cup dried apples, chopped

Combine all ingredients in a large bowl until well blended. Recipe makes 4-1/4 cups of mix. Place mix in a plastic zipper-type bag. Place bag inside a homespun fabric gift bag (see page 56 for instructions). Tie top closed with raffia and attach a wooden spoon and cooking instruction tag.

Gift basket idea for a first-time home owner: Place fabric bag of mix inside a mixing bowl that is filled with colorful paper shred. Add two pot holders, a set of measuring cups and measuring spoons and a bottle of vanilla extract.

Apple Walnut Muffin Mix

To Prepare: In a large mixing bowl, combine mix, one slightly beaten egg, 3/4 cup milk, 1 teaspoon vanilla extract and 1/4 cup vegetable oil. Stir just until moistened. Fill greased muffin tins 3/4 full. Bake at 400° until golden brown, about 15-18 minutes. Makes 12 muffins.

Chocolate Cherry Nut Muffin Mix in a Jar

2 cups self-rising flour
1/3 cup brown sugar, gently packed
1/2 cup granulated sugar
3/4 cup dried, sweetened cherries, chopped
1/3 cup chopped nuts
1/3 cup chocolate chips

Pour the flour into a 1-quart wide-mouth canning jar. Tap gently on a lightly padded surface on the counter to settle. Sprinkle the brown sugar over the flour and press down gently to pack. Pour the granulated sugar over the brown sugar and tap jar gently to settle. Sprinkle cherry pieces over granulated sugar and press down gently to pack. Add the nuts and chocolate chips, tapping the jar gently on the counter after each layer to settle ingredients. Add the lid.

Decorate the jar lid with a fabric circle as described on page 59 and attach the cooking instruction tag:

Chocolate Cherry Nut Muffin Mix

To Prepare: Preheat oven to 350°. Empty contents of jar into a large bowl and stir to blend. In a separate bowl, blend 1 large egg, 1/2 cup (1 stick) melted butter and 1 cup milk. Add egg mixture to muffin mix and stir just until moistened. Spoon batter into 12 greased muffin cups. Bake 15-18 minutes or until done.

Apricot Nut Bread Mix

2-1/2 cups biscuit baking mix
1/4 cup brown sugar, packed
1/2 cup granulated sugar
1 teaspoon ground cinnamon
3/4 cup dried apricots, chopped
1/2 cup walnuts, chopped

Combine all ingredients in a large bowl until well blended. Recipe makes 4-1/2 cups mix. Place mix in a plastic zipper-type bag. Place bag inside a fabric gift bag (see page 56 for instructions). Tie top closed with ribbon or raffia. Or place in a paper gift bag (see page 57 for ideas). Attach a wooden spoon and cooking instruction tag to bow.

Gift basket idea: Place bag of bread mix inside a loaf pan that is lined with a tea towel. Include an oven mitt or two pot holders.

Apricot Nut Bread Mix

To Prepare: Preheat oven to 350°. Empty mix into a large bowl. In a separate bowl, blend 2 large eggs, 1/4 cup (1/2 stick) melted butter, 1 teaspoon vanilla extract and 3/4 cup milk. Add egg mixture to bread mix and stir just until moistened. Spoon batter into a greased 9" x 5" loaf pan. Bake for 45-50 minutes or until done. Cool in pan on wire rack before removing.

Rich Chocolate Gravy Mix

1-1/2 cups granulated sugar
3 tablespoons cornstarch
1-1/2 tablespoons unsweetened
    cocoa powder
1/4 teaspoon salt

In a medium bowl, combine all
ingredients until well blended.
Recipe makes about 1-3/4 cups of
mix. Place mix in a plastic zipper-
type bag. Place plastic bag inside a fabric gift bag (see page
56 for instructions) and tie closed with ribbon, raffia or
jute. Or place in a paper gift bag (see page 57 for ideas).
Attach a wire whisk or small wooden spoon and cooking
instruction tag to bow.

For a gift basket idea: Place a fabric gift bag of gravy mix
and a fabric gift bag of Angel Biscuit Mix (page 53) inside
a basket that is filled with colorful paper shred.

Rich Chocolate Gravy Mix

To Prepare: In a large saucepan,
blend gravy mix with 3 cups of
milk. Cook over medium heat,
stirring constantly, until mixture
thickens. Remove from heat and
add 1 teaspoon vanilla extract.
Serve over hot buttered biscuits.

Brownie & Cookie Mixes

Cowboy Cookie Mix

1-1/3 cups all purpose flour
1-1/3 cups quick cooking oats
1/2 teaspoon baking powder
1 teaspoon baking soda
1/4 teaspoon salt
1/2 cup brown sugar, packed
1/2 cup granulated sugar
1/2 cup pecans, chopped
1/2 cup sweetened, flaked coconut
1 cup semi-sweet chocolate chips

In a large bowl, combine all ingredients until well blended. Place mix in a plastic zipper-type bag. Place bag in the center of a red bandana. Draw corners together and tie closed with jute or raffia. Attach cooking instruction tag.

Cowboy Cookie Mix

To Prepare: Preheat oven to 350°. Empty mix into a large bowl. Add 1/2 cup (1 stick) butter or margarine, melted; 1 egg, slightly beaten; and 1 teaspoon vanilla extract. Stir to blend thoroughly. Shape into walnut-size balls and place on a greased baking sheet about 2" apart. Bake for 11-13 minutes or until edges are lightly browned. Cool 5 minutes on baking sheet then remove to racks to cool completely. Makes about 3 dozen cookies.

Tangy Orange Cookie Mix in a Jar

1-3/4 cups all-purpose flour
1/2 teaspoon baking soda
1/2 teaspoon baking powder
1/4 teaspoon salt
1/2 cup orange flavored instant breakfast drink powder
3/4 cup granulated sugar
1-1/2 cups vanilla baking chips

Combine flour, baking soda, baking powder and salt. Pour flour mixture into a 1-quart wide-mouth canning jar. Tap jar gently on lightly padded surface on the counter to settle. Layer remaining ingredients in order listed, tapping jar gently on the counter to settle each layer before adding next ingredient. Add the jar lid. Decorate the lid with a fabric circle as described on page 59 and attach the cooking instruction tag.

Tangy Orange Cookie Mix

To Prepare: Preheat oven to 375°. Empty contents of jar into a large bowl and stir to blend. Add 1/2 cup (1 stick) butter or margarine, softened; 1 egg, slightly beaten; and 1 teaspoon vanilla extract. Stir to blend thoroughly. Roll heaping tablespoonfuls into balls. Place 2" apart on a lightly greased baking sheet. Bake for 12-14 minutes or until tops are very lightly browned. Cool 5 minutes on cookie sheet. Remove to wire racks to cool completely. Makes about 2-1/2 dozen.

Coconut Almond Cookies

2 cups biscuit baking mix
1 cup brown sugar, packed
1 cup sweetened, flaked coconut
1/2 cup sliced almonds

In a large bowl, combine all ingredients until well blended. Recipe makes about 4-1/2 cups of mix. Place mix in a plastic zipper-type bag. Place plastic bag inside a fabric gift bag (see page 56 for instructions) and tie closed with ribbon, raffia or jute.

Or place in a paper gift bag (see page 57 for ideas). Attach cooking instruction tag and a wooden spoon.

Coconut Almond Cookie Mix

To Prepare: Preheat oven to 375°. Pour cookie mix into a large bowl. Add 1/2 cup melted butter or margarine, 1 large egg and 1 teaspoon vanilla extract. Stir until well blended. Roll into 1" balls and place about 2" apart on a greased cookie sheet. Bake 10-12 minutes or until lightly browned. Cool 5 minutes on baking sheet then remove to racks to cool completely. Makes about 2-1/2 dozen cookies.

Crunchy Toffee Cookie Mix

2/3 cup toffee chips
1/2 cup chopped pecans
1 cup brown sugar, packed
2 cups biscuit baking mix

In a large bowl, blend all ingredients together. Recipe makes about 4 cups of mix. Place mix in a plastic zipper-type bag. Place plastic bag inside a fabric gift bag (see page 56 for instructions) and tie closed with ribbon, raffia or jute. Or place in a paper gift bag (see page 57 for ideas). Attach cooking instruction tag.

For a gift basket idea for a new home owner: Place the fabric bag of cookie mix in a mixing bowl that is filled with paper shred. Add a wooden spoon, a set of measuring spoons, two pot holders and a small bottle of vanilla extract.

Crunchy Toffee Cookie Mix

To Prepare: Preheat oven to 375°. Pour mix into a large bowl. Add 1/2 cup (1 stick) butter or margarine, melted; 1 large egg, slightly beaten; and 1 teaspoon vanilla extract. Stir to blend thoroughly. Shape into 1" balls. Place 2" apart on lightly greased baking sheets. Bake 10-12 minutes or until lightly browned. Cool 5 minutes on cookie sheet. Remove to wire racks to cool completely. Makes about 2-1/2 dozen cookies.

Oatmeal Raisin Cookie Mix

2 cups quick-cooking oats
1 cup all-purpose flour
3/4 cup brown sugar, firmly packed
1/2 cup granulated sugar
1 teaspoon ground cinnamon
1 teaspoon baking soda
1/4 teaspoon salt
3/4 cup raisins

In a large bowl, combine all ingredients until well blended. Recipe makes about 5 cups of mix. Place mix in a plastic zipper-type bag. Place plastic bag inside a fabric gift bag (see page 56 for instructions) and tie closed with ribbon, raffia or jute. Or place in a paper gift bag (see page 57 for ideas). Attach cooking instruction tag.

Oatmeal Raisin Cookie Mix

To Prepare: Preheat oven to 350°. Pour mix into a large bowl. Add 3/4 cup butter or margarine, softened; 1 egg, slightly beaten; and 1 teaspoon vanilla extract. Stir to blend thoroughly. Shape into walnut-size balls and place on a greased baking sheet about 2" apart. Bake for 11-13 minutes or until edges are lightly browned. Cool 5 minutes on baking sheet then remove to racks to cool completely. Makes about 3 dozen cookies.

Peanut Butter Cup Cookie Mix in a Jar

3/4 cup granulated sugar
1/2 cup brown sugar, packed
1-3/4 cups all-purpose flour
1 teaspoon baking powder
1/2 teaspoon baking soda
1/4 teaspoon salt
20 mini peanut butter cups, chopped

Pour granulated sugar into a 1-quart, wide mouth canning jar. Tap gently on a padded surface on the counter to settle ingredients. Sprinkle brown sugar over granulated sugar and press down to pack. Combine flour, baking powder, baking soda and salt in a small bowl. Pour over brown sugar and tap gently to settle. Wrap peanut butter cups in plastic wrap and place on top of flour mixture. Add the jar lid. Decorate the jar lid with a fabric circle as described on page 59 and attach the cooking instruction tag.

Peanut Butter Cup Cookie Mix

To Prepare: Preheat oven to 350°. Remove peanut butter cups from jar and set aside. Empty remaining contents of jar into a large bowl and stir to blend. Add 1/2 cup (1 stick) butter or margarine, softened; 1 egg, slightly beaten; and 1 teaspoon vanilla extract. Mix to blend thoroughly. Stir in peanut butter cups. Shape into walnut-size balls and place on a greased baking sheet about 2" apart. Bake 12-14 minutes or until edges are lightly browned. Cool 5 minutes on baking sheet then remove to wire racks to cool completely. Makes about 2-1/2 dozen cookies.

Coconut Pecan Blondie Mix in a Jar

1-3/4 cups all-purpose flour
1 teaspoon baking powder
1/4 teaspoon salt
1-3/4 cups brown sugar, gently packed
1/2 cup sweetened, flaked coconut, gently packed
1/2 cup chopped pecans

Mix together flour, baking powder and salt. Pour flour mixture into a 1-quart wide-mouth canning jar. Tap jar gently on lightly padded surface on the counter to settle flour. Sprinkle brown sugar over flour mixture and press down gently to pack. Sprinkle coconut over brown sugar and press down gently to pack. Sprinkle pecans over coconut and tap jar gently on the counter to settle nuts. Add the jar lid

Decorate jar with fabric circle as described on page 59 and attach cooking instruction tag.

Coconut Pecan Blondie Mix

To Prepare: Preheat oven to 350°. Empty contents of jar into a large bowl and stir to mix. In a separate bowl, blend 2/3 cup melted butter or margarine, 2 large eggs and 1 teaspoon vanilla extract. Add egg mixture to mix and stir until well blended. Spread batter in a greased 9" square baking pan. Bake for about 25-30 minutes or until done. Cool completely in pan before cutting into squares.

Mocha Fudge Brownie Mix

1 cup all-purpose flour
1/2 teaspoon baking powder
1/2 teaspoon salt
1/2 cup unsweetened cocoa powder
3/4 cup granulated sugar
3/4 cup brown sugar, gently packed
1/2 cup semi-sweet chocolate chips
3/4 cup chopped pecans
1 bottle (50 ml) coffee-flavored liqueur

In a large bowl, combine all ingredients except liqueur. Recipe makes about 4-1/4 cups of mix. Place mix in a plastic zipper-type bag. Place plastic bag inside a fabric gift bag (see page 56 for instructions) and tie closed with ribbon, raffia or jute. Or place in a paper gift bag (see page 57 for ideas). Attach bottle of liqueur and cooking instruction tag to bow.

Mocha Fudge Brownie Mix

To Prepare: Preheat oven to 350º. Pour mix into a large bowl. In a separate bowl, blend 2 large eggs, 1/2 cup (1 stick) melted butter and liqueur. Add egg mixture to brownie mix and stir just until moistened. Spread batter in a greased 9" square pan. Bake for 30 to 35 minutes or until toothpick inserted in center comes out almost clean. Cool completely in pan before cutting into squares.

Other Dessert Mixes

Funnel Cake Mix

1 cup all-purpose flour
1 teaspoon baking powder
1/4 teaspoon salt
1/2 teaspoon ground cinnamon

Combine all ingredients until well blended. Recipe makes about 1 cup of mix. Place in a plastic zipper-type bag. Place plastic bag inside a fabric gift bag and tie closed with jute or raffia (see page 56 for instructions) or a paper gift bag (see page 57). Attach a small whisk and cooking instruction tag.

For a gift basket idea: Place fabric bag of mix inside a basket or small, deep skillet and include a funnel and a shaker container filled with powdered sugar for sprinkling on the cakes.

Funnel Cake Mix

To Prepare: Pour vegetable oil into a skillet to depth of 1". Heat oil to 360° over medium-high heat. In a small bowl, combine 1 egg with 3/4 cup milk. Add mix and beat with a fork or whisk until smooth. Holding finger under funnel opening, pour about 1/4 cup batter into funnel. Allow batter to pour from funnel into hot oil, moving funnel in a circle to form a spiral shape. Fry 1 minute, turn cake and continue frying until golden brown. Remove to paper towels to drain. Sprinkle with powdered sugar. Makes 6 funnel cakes.

Microwave Brownie Pie Mix

1 cup granulated sugar
1/2 cup all-purpose flour
1/2 cup chopped pecans
3 tablespoons unsweetened cocoa powder
1/4 teaspoon salt

Combine all ingredients until well blended. Recipe makes about 2 cups of mix. Place mix in a plastic zipper-type bag. Place plastic bag inside a fabric gift bag (see page 56 for instructions) and tie closed with raffia or jute. Or place in a paper gift bag (see page 57 for ideas). Attach cooking instruction tag.

For a gift basket idea: Place fabric bag of mix inside a pie plate with a pie server.

Microwave Brownie Pie Mix

To Prepare: Empty mix into a medium bowl. Stir in 1/2 cup melted butter or margarine, 2 eggs and 1 teaspoon vanilla extract until well blended. Pour batter into a greased 9" microwave-safe pie plate. Microwave on 60% power 10-12 minutes or until almost set in the center. Do not over bake. Serve warm with ice cream. Makes 8 servings.

German Chocolate Cake Mix in a Jar

1-1/2 cups all-purpose flour
2 teaspoons baking powder
1/4 teaspoon salt
1/2 cup unsweetened cocoa powder
1/2 cup granulated sugar
1/4 cup brown sugar, gently packed
1/2 cup semi-sweet chocolate chips
1/2 cup pecans, chopped
1/2 cup sweetened, flaked coconut, gently
packed

Combine flour, baking powder and salt. Pour flour mixture into a 1-quart wide-mouth canning jar. Tap jar gently on lightly padded surface on the counter to settle. Add cocoa and then granulated sugar, tapping jar gently on the counter after each layer to settle. Sprinkle brown sugar over granulated sugar and press down gently to pack. Add chocolate chips and then pecans, tapping jar gently after each layer to settle. Place coconut over pecans and press down gently to pack. Add the lid. Decorate jar lid with a fabric circle as described on page 59 and attach cooking instruction tag.

German Chocolate Cake Mix

To Prepare: Preheat oven to 350°. Empty contents of jar into a large bowl and stir to blend. In a separate bowl, blend 2 large eggs, 1/4 cup melted butter, 1 teaspoon vanilla extract and 3/4 cup milk. Add egg mixture to cake mix and stir just until moistened. Pour batter into a greased 9" square baking pan. Bake 25-30 minutes or until done. Cool in pan and cut into squares to serve.

S' Mores Mix

2 cups of coarsely crushed graham crackers
2 cups of miniature marshmallows
1 cup of semi-sweet or milk chocolate chips

In a large bowl, combine all ingredients until well blended. Place about 1-1/4 cups mix in each of four clear or printed cellophane treat bags.

Close with a bow tied around the top using 1" wide wired ribbon. Attach cooking instruction tag when tying bow. Place each bag of mix inside a mug.

S' Mores Mix
To Prepare: Empty mix into mug. Microwave on high power for 30-45 seconds, or until marshmallows are puffed and melted. Let stand in microwave 2 minutes to soften chocolate chips. Enjoy.

Coconut Cream Pudding Mix

1-1/2 cups instant nonfat dry milk
2 cups granulated sugar
1-1/2 cups cornstarch
1/2 teaspoon salt
2 cups shredded, unsweetened
   coconut
1/2 teaspoon coconut extract

In a large bowl, combine dry milk, sugar, cornstarch and salt. Process coconut and coconut extract in a blender for 1 minute. Add to cornstarch mixture and stir until well blended. Recipe makes 6 cups. Place 2/3 cup of mix into 9 plastic bags.

Place each bag of mix in a colorful paper sack. Fold a paper doily in half and cover top edge of sack. Punch two holes about 1" apart and 1/2" down from the top of the folded edge of the doily through all layers. Thread each end of a piece of ribbon through the holes from the back to the front and tie a bow at the front of the sack. Attach the cooking instruction tag before tying the ribbon into a bow. Trim ends of ribbon to desired length.

Coconut Cream Pudding Mix

To prepare: Pour mix into a saucepan. Add 2 cups milk and cook over medium low heat, stirring until mixture thickens and comes to a boil. Continue stirring 1 minute. Remove from heat and pour into 4 individual serving dishes. Pudding will thicken more as it cools.

Lemon Dessert Mix

2-1/2 cups presweetened
    powdered lemonade mix
1 cup plus 2 tablespoons
    cornstarch
1-1/4 cups granulated sugar
1 teaspoon salt

In a large bowl, combine all ingredients until well blended. Recipe makes 4 cups of mix. Divide mix evenly between two one-pint, wide-mouth canning jars. Add jar lids. Decorate each jar lid with a fabric circle as described on page 59. Fold cooking instruction tag in half, punch a hole where marked, write "Lemon Dessert Mix" on the front and attach tag to ribbon.

Lemon Dessert Mix

To Make Hot Lemon Sauce: Combine 1 cup water and 1/4 cup Lemon Mix in a small saucepan. Bring to a boil, stirring constantly until thickened. Remove from heat. Add 2 tablespoons butter. Serve warm over gingerbread, pound cake or other desserts.

- -

To Make Lemon Pie: In a large saucepan, combine 1-1/4 cups Lemon Mix, 1/2 cup water and 3 egg yolks. Mix until smooth. Add 2 more cups water. Cook over medium heat until thick and bubbly; stirring constantly. Remove from heat. Add 2 tablespoons butter. Cover and let cool for 5 minutes. Stir and pour into baked pie crust or graham cracker crust. Cover and refrigerate for 3 hours. Top with sweetened whipped cream or non-dairy whipped topping.

Holiday Snack Mix

These festive little bags make great party favors.

2 (10 oz.) packages miniature peanut butter sandwich
    cookies
2 (6 oz.) packages sweetened dried cranberries
1 (16 oz.) package red and green candy-coated chocolate
    pieces
2 (10 oz.) packages buttery toffee popcorn with peanuts

In a large bowl, combine all ingredients. Recipe makes
about 22 cups of snack mix. Place about 1 cup of snack mix
in a cellophane bag (clear or printed with Holiday designs)
and tie closed with a colorful ribbon bow.

Attach label before tying bow.

Halloween Snack Mix

These festive little bags make great party favors.

2 (7-1/2 oz.) packages chocolate-covered pretzels
1 (8-1/2 oz.) package mini chocolate chip cookies
1 (16 oz.) package candy-coated peanut butter pieces
2 cups small orange slice candies

Combine all ingredients in a large bowl until well blended. Recipe makes about 13 cups of mix. Place about 1 cup of snack mix in a cellophane bag (clear or printed with Halloween designs) and tie closed with an orange and black ribbon bow.

Attach label before tying bow.

Halloween
Snack Mix

Chocolate Mint Cheese Ball Mix

1 (12 oz.) package semi-sweet chocolate chips
2 cups chopped pecans
1 cup of 1-inch diameter peppermint candies (about 36)

Finely grind all ingredients in a blender or food processor. Makes about 6 cups of mix. Place about 1-1/2 cups mix into each of 4 separate plastic zipper-type bags. Place each plastic bag inside a fabric gift bag (see page 56 for instructions) and tie closed with raffia or jute. Attach the cooking instruction tag and a cheese spreader to the bow. Or place in a paper gift bag (see page 57 for ideas) or a colorful Chinese take-out container.

For a gift basket idea, place bag of mix in a small basket along with an attractive cheese serving tray and a clear cellophane bag filled with chocolate wafer cookies and tied with a bow.

Chocolate Mint Cheese Ball Mix

To Prepare: Stir 1-1/2 cups mix into one 8 oz. package of softened cream cheese. Shape into a ball; wrap in plastic wrap and refrigerate until firm. To serve, let stand at room temperature 20-30 minutes or until softened. Serve with chocolate wafer cookies. Makes 1 cheese ball.

Chocolate-Cinnamon Popcorn Spice Mix

1/2 cup powdered sugar
1/4 cup semi-sweet chocolate
   chips, chilled and finely
   ground in a food processor
2 tablespoons unsweetened cocoa
   powder
1/2 teaspoon ground cinnamon

Combine all ingredients until well blended. Recipe makes about 3/4 cup of mix. Place mix in a small glass canister with an airtight, hinged lid or in a decorative tin. Attach cooking instruction tag.

Gift basket idea: Place a jar of spice mix in a large popcorn bowl that is filled with colorful paper shred, along with several bags of microwaveable popcorn.

Chocolate-Cinnamon Popcorn Spice Mix

To Prepare: Melt 1/4 cup butter in a small saucepan over low heat. Stir in 2 tablespoons spice mix. Pour over 3 cups of popped corn. Stir well.

Seasoning & Dip Mixes

Dilly Dip Mix

1/4 cup dried dill weed
1/4 cup dried parsley flakes
1/4 cup dried minced onion
2 tablespoons seasoned salt

In a small bowl, combine all ingredients until well blended. Divide into 9 tiny plastic bags—each one containing 1-1/2 tablespoons of dip mix. If you can't find tiny bags, wrap each portion of mix in a double layer of plastic wrap

Gift giving idea: Place each bag of mix inside the bowl of a wooden spoon. Using pinking shears, cut a 10" square of fabric and wrap it around the spoon bowl and dip mix bag. Gather fabric around neck of spoon and tie with ribbon or raffia. Attach cooking instruction tag.

Dilly Dip Mix
To Prepare: In a small bowl, combine half a cup of mayonnaise and half a cup of sour cream with 1-1/2 tablespoons dill mix. Stir until well blended and chill two hours before serving.

Garden Herb Bread Seasoning

1/3 cup dried parsley flakes
1/3 cup dried minced onion
2-1/2 tablespoons dried basil leaves, crushed
2-1/2 teaspoons dried thyme leaves
2-1/2 teaspoons dried oregano leaves
1-1/4 teaspoon garlic powder

In a small bowl, blend all ingredients together. Recipe makes about 1 cup of seasoning. Place about 1/4 cup of mix into each of four small zipper-type bags. Bundle each plastic bag inside a 10" square of fabric and tie closed with raffia or jute. Attach cooking instruction tag. Place bundle inside a small terracotta flower pot filled with paper shred.

For a gift basket idea, place a bundle of seasoning blend in a flower pot along with a bag of Beer Bread Mix (page 51).

Garden Herb Bread Seasoning

To Use: Add one tablespoon seasoning blend to a package of hot roll mix or your favorite quick bread recipe. Prepare and bake bread as directed on package or recipe.

Cinnamon-Citrus Marinade Mix

3 tablespoons brown sugar, packed
1 teaspoon dried, grated orange peel
1 teaspoon ground cinnamon
1/2 teaspoon ground nutmeg
1/2 teaspoon salt
1/4 teaspoon ground black pepper

In a small bowl, combine all ingredients until well blended. Recipe makes about 1/4 cup of mix. Place mix in a small plastic zipper-type bag. Place bag of mix in the center of a 10" square of fabric. Gather the fabric around the mix and tie with ribbon, jute or raffia. Attach cooking instruction tag before tying ribbon into a bow.

Gift basket idea: Place the fabric bundle of marinade mix in a basket that is filled with paper shred. Add a meat thermometer, pair of tongs and an oven mitt.

Cinnamon-Citrus Marinade Mix

To Use: Combine 1 tablespoon marinade mix with 1/4 cup vegetable or olive oil & 1/4 cup orange juice. Marinate beef, chicken or pork for at least one hour before grilling or roasting.

Barbecue Seasoning Blend

2 tablespoons dried parsley flakes
3 tablespoons onion powder
3 tablespoons garlic powder
2 tablespoons celery salt
2 tablespoons dry mustard
1 tablespoon black pepper

In a small bowl, blend all ingredients together. Recipe makes about 3/4 cup of seasoning blend. Place about 1/4 cup of blend into three small zipper-type bags. Bundle each plastic bag inside a 10" square of fabric and tie closed with raffia or jute.

Or place plastic bag of mix inside a small gift sack. Fold the top down about 1". Punch two holes about 1" apart in the center of the fold. Thread each end of a length of raffia or jute through the holes from back to front. Tie the ends into a bow at the front and trim ends. Attach cooking instruction tag.

For a gift basket idea, place a bag of seasoning blend in a basket with an oven mitt and a pair of grilling tongs.

Barbecue
Seasoning Blend

Sprinkle generously on beef, pork or fish before grilling or broiling.

Fish Fry Seasoning

2 cups yellow cornmeal
1 cup all-purpose flour
2 teaspoons paprika
1 teaspoon dried parsley flakes
1 teaspoon salt
1 teaspoon celery salt
1 teaspoon onion powder
1 teaspoon lemon pepper
1/2 teaspoon ground red pepper

In a large bowl, combine all ingredients until well blended. Recipe makes about 3 cups of mix (enough to coat about 4 pounds of fish). Place in a plastic zipper-type bag. Place plastic bag inside a fabric gift bag (see page 56 for instructions) and tie closed with jute or raffia, or place bag of mix inside a paper gift bag (see page 57 for ideas). Attach cooking instruction tag.

For a gift basket idea, place the fabric bag inside a small skillet, along with a bag of hush puppy mix (page 54).

Fish Fry Seasoning

To Prepare: Heat about 1-1/2 inches vegetable oil to 375° in a deep skillet. In a small bowl, combine 1 egg and 1 cup buttermilk. Dip fish filets into buttermilk mixture. Roll in fish fry seasoning until well coated. Fry until fish is golden brown and flakes easily with a fork. Drain on paper towels.

Salad Sprinkles

2/3 cup shoestring potato
  sticks
1/2 cup roasted sunflower
  seeds
2 tablespoons imitation bacon
  bits
2 tablespoons sesame seeds
2 tablespoons salad seasoning
  (found in the grocery store spice section)
1 teaspoon Italian seasoning

Break potato sticks into small pieces. Combine with remaining ingredients. Recipe makes about 1-1/2 cups of mix. Place in a plastic zipper-type bag. Place plastic bag inside a fabric gift bag and tie closed with jute or raffia (see page 56 for instructions) or a paper gift bag (see page 57) for ideas. Or place plastic bag of mix in a decorative tin or colorful Chinese take-out container (found at craft stores). Attach cooking instruction tag.

Gift Giving Idea: Place fabric bag or decorative tin of salad sprinkles inside a stack of four salad bowls along with four fabric napkins.

Salad Sprinkles

To Serve: Sprinkle
generously over tossed
green salads.

Seasoned Salt Blend

1 cup salt
2 teaspoons granulated sugar
2 teaspoons dry mustard
1-1/2 teaspoons garlic powder
1 teaspoon ground oregano
1 teaspoon curry powder
1 teaspoon onion powder
1/4 teaspoon paprika
1/4 teaspoon ground thyme

In a small bowl, mix all ingredients together until well blended. Recipe makes about 1-1/4 cups seasoning blend. Divide evenly between two plastic zipper type bags or airtight containers. Place each plastic bag inside a fabric gift bag and tie closed with jute or raffia (see page 56 for instructions) or a paper gift sack (see page 57 for ideas). Or place in a decorative tin or canister with an airtight lid. Attach label.

Gift Basket Idea: Place a gift bag of seasoned salt and a gift bag of seasoned pepper in a basket filled with paper shred, along with a pair of cute salt and pepper shakers.

Seasoned Salt

Seasoned Pepper Blend

1/3 cup whole black peppercorns
3 tablespoons sweet pepper flakes
2 tablespoons whole white peppercorns
1 teaspoon dried minced onion
1 teaspoon crushed red pepper flakes
1/2 teaspoon dried minced garlic

Place all ingredients in a food processor or blender and process to a coarse powder. Recipe makes about 2/3 cups seasoning blend. Place 1/3 cup of seasoning into each of two plastic zipper type bags. Place plastic bag inside a fabric gift bag (see page 56 for instructions) and tie closed with jute or raffia. Or place plastic bag of pepper in a paper gift sack (see page 57). Or place in a decorative tin or canister with an airtight lid. Attach label.

Gift Basket Idea: Place a gift bag of seasoned salt and a gift bag of seasoned pepper in a basket filled with paper shred, along with a pair of cute salt and pepper shakers.

Seasoned Pepper

Soup Mixes

Creamy Potato Soup Mix

1-3/4 cup instant mashed potato flakes

1-1/2 cups instant nonfat dry milk

2 tablespoons chicken bouillon granules

2 teaspoons dried, minced onion

2 teaspoons seasoned salt

2 teaspoons dried parsley flakes

1/2 teaspoon dried thyme

1/4 teaspoon ground black pepper

Combine all ingredients in a large mixing bowl. Recipe makes about 4 cups of mix. Place in a one-quart, wide-mouth canning jar; seal with lid. Decorate jar with fabric circle as described on page 59 and attach cooking instruction tag.

Gift Giving Idea: Place individual servings of soup mix (1/2 cup) into small zipper-type bags. Place each bag in the center of a 12" square of homespun fabric. Gather the fabric around the mix and tie with jute or raffia. Attach cooking instruction tag. Place inside a mug or soup bowl.

Creamy Potato Soup Mix

To Prepare: Combine 1/2 cup of mix with 1 cup boiling water in a bowl or mug. Stir until smooth. Makes 1 serving.

Country Chicken Noodle Soup in a Jar

1 package (2.75 ounces) country gravy mix
2 tablespoons chicken bouillon granules
2 tablespoons dried minced onion
2 tablespoons dried celery flakes
2 teaspoons dried parsley flakes
2-1/2 to 3 cups uncooked wide egg noodles

Pour gravy mix into wide-mouth 1-quart canning jar. In a small bowl, stir together bouillon, onion, celery and parsley. Pour seasoning mixture into jar over gravy mix. Add the noodles. Attach the lid. Decorate jar with a fabric circle as described on page 59 and attach cooking instruction tag.

Gift basket idea: Place the jar of soup mix in a basket that is lined with a tea towel, along with a 10-oz. can of chicken and a fabric gift bag filled with a bag of Cranberry Cornbread Muffin Mix (page 52).

Country Chicken Noodle Soup Mix

To Prepare: Empty mix into a 4-quart saucepan. Add 8 cups water; heat to boiling over medium-high heat. Stir in one 10-ounce or two 5-ounce cans of cooked and chopped chicken. Cover and simmer 5-6 minutes or until noodles are tender, stirring occasionally. Makes 6 servings.

Corn Chowder Mix for Two

6 tablespoons instant mashed potato flakes
2 tablespoons instant nonfat dry milk
2 teaspoons imitation bacon bits
2 teaspoons dried celery flakes
1 teaspoon chicken bouillon granules
1 teaspoon instant minced onion
1/4 teaspoon seasoned salt
Dash of ground black pepper

In a small bowl, combine all ingredients. Recipe makes about 2/3 cup of mix. Place in a small plastic zipper-type bag. Place plastic bag inside a fabric gift bag and tie closed with ribbon, jute or raffia (see page 56 for instructions) or a paper gift bag (see page 57 for ideas). Attach cooking instruction tag.

Additional ingredients: One (8 oz.) can cream style corn

For a gift basket idea: Place the fabric bag of mix, a can of cream style corn and two mugs in a basket that is lined with two fabric napkins

Corn Chowder Mix for Two
To Prepare: Empty mix into a small saucepan. Add 1 cup of water, 2 teaspoons butter or margarine and one 8 oz. can of cream style corn. Bring to a boil over medium-high heat. Cover and simmer 5 minutes, stirring occasionally.

Chicken Tortilla Soup Mix

1 cup coarsely crushed Cool Ranch flavor tortilla chips
1/2 cup uncooked instant rice
1 (1.4 oz.) package of dry vegetable soup mix
4 teaspoons chicken bouillon granules
1/2 teaspoon garlic powder
1/2 teaspoon ground cumin
1/4 teaspoon ground black pepper

In a medium bowl, combine all ingredients. Recipe makes about 2 cups of mix. Place mix in a plastic zipper-type bag. Place plastic bag inside a fabric gift bag and tie closed with ribbon, jute or raffia (see page 56 for instructions) or a paper gift bag (see page 57 for ideas). Attach cooking instruction tag.

Additional ingredients: Two (5 oz.) cans cooked chicken

For a gift basket idea: Place the fabric bag of mix, a small bag of tortilla chips and 2 cans of chicken in a basket that is lined with a fabric napkin.

Chicken Tortilla Soup Mix

To Prepare: Empty mix into a large saucepan. Add 5 cups of water and two 5 oz. cans of cooked chicken, drained. Bring to a boil over medium-high heat. Cover and simmer 10 minutes, stirring occasionally. Serve with extra tortilla chips. Serves 4.

Biscuit & Bread Mixes

Beer Bread Mix

3 cups self-rising flour
1/3 cup granulated sugar

In a large bowl, combine ingredients until well blended.

Place mix in a plastic zipper-type bag. Place plastic bag inside a fabric gift bag and tie closed with jute or raffia (see page 56 for instructions) or a paper gift bag (see page 57 for ideas). Attach cooking tag.

For a gift basket idea, place the fabric bag of mix inside a loaf pan along with a can of beer and an oven mitt. Or place it in a terracotta flower pot with a bag of Garden Herb Bread Seasoning (page 40).

Beer Bread Mix

To Prepare: Preheat oven to 350º. Place mix in large bowl and add one 12 oz. can of beer (at room temperature) and 2 tablespoons melted butter or margarine. Blend just until ingredients are moistened. Pour into a greased and floured 9" X 5" loaf pan. Bake for 50 minutes or until done. Remove from pan and cool on a wire rack. Serve warm.

Cranberry Cornbread Muffin Mix in a Jar

2 cups biscuit baking mix
3/4 cup brown sugar, gently packed
2/3 cup yellow corn meal
3/4 cup dried cranberries, chopped

Pour baking mix into a 1-quart wide-mouth canning jar. Tap gently on a lightly padded surface on the counter to settle. Sprinkle brown sugar over baking mix and press down gently to pack. Pour cornmeal over brown sugar and tap jar gently to settle. Add cranberries and press down gently to pack. Decorate jar with a fabric circle as described on page 59 and attach cooking instructions.

Gift basket idea: Place muffin mix in a plastic bag instead of a jar and place in a fabric gift bag (instructions on page 56). Place the bag of mix in a basket lined with a tea towel, along with a jar of Country Chicken Noodle Soup Mix (page 48) or Creamy Potato Soup Mix (page 47).

Cranberry Cornbread Muffin Mix

To Prepare: Preheat oven to 375°. Empty contents of jar into a large bowl and stir to mix. In a separate bowl, blend 1 large egg, 1/2 cup (1 stick) melted butter and 1 cup milk. Add egg mixture to muffin mix and stir just until moistened. Spoon batter into 12 greased muffin cups. Bake for 18-20 minutes or until done.

Angel Biscuit Mix

2-1/2 cups biscuit baking mix
1/2 cup sweetened, flaked coconut

In a large bowl, blend together baking mix and coconut. Place in a plastic zipper-type bag. Place plastic bag inside a fabric gift bag and tie closed with jute or raffia (see page 56 for instructions) or a paper gift bag (see page 57 for ideas). Attach cooking instruction tag and a biscuit cutter.

For a gift basket idea, place the fabric bag of mix inside a mixing bowl that is lined with a tea towel and filled with colorful paper shred. Include a jar of flavored honey or a bag of Rich Chocolate Gravy Mix (page 20) and a wooden spoon.

Angel Biscuit Mix

To Prepare: Preheat oven to 450°. Empty mix into a large bowl. Stir in 1 cup heavy cream, just until moistened. Turn dough out onto a lightly floured surface and knead gently 10-12 strokes or until smooth. Pat dough to 1/2" thickness. Cut out biscuits using a 2" biscuit cutter and place 2" apart on a greased baking sheet. Brush tops with melted butter. Bake 7-10 minutes or until done. Serve warm with butter. Makes about 1-1/2 dozen biscuits.

Hush Puppy Mix

1-1/2 cups yellow cornmeal
3/4 cup all-purpose flour
3 tablespoons dried mined onion
1 teaspoon baking powder
1 teaspoon granulated sugar
1 teaspoon salt
1/2 teaspoon baking soda
1/4 teaspoon garlic powder
1/4 teaspoon ground red pepper

In a medium bowl, combine all ingredients. Recipe makes about 2-1/4 cups mix. Place mix in a plastic zipper-type bag. Place plastic bag inside a fabric gift bag and tie closed with jute or raffia (see page 56 for instructions) or a paper gift bag (see page 57 for ideas). Attach cooking instruction tag.

For a gift basket idea, place the fabric bag of mix inside a small skillet along with a bag of fish fry seasoning mix (page 43).

Hush Puppy Mix

To Prepare: Heat about 1-1/2 inches of vegetable oil to 350° in a deep skillet. In a medium bowl, combine 1-1/4 cups buttermilk, 1 slightly beaten egg and mix; stir until well blended. Drop batter by tablespoonfuls into hot oil. Fry until golden brown on both sides and fully cooked. Drain on paper towels. Serve warm. Makes about 3 dozen.

Packaging & Decorating Your Gifts From the Kitchen

Making Fabric Gift Bags

To make fabric gift bags, cut two pieces of fabric:

5" wide X 7" high	(for 1/2 cup of mix)
5-1/2" wide X 8-1/2" high	(for 1 cup of mix)
6" wide X 10" high	(for 2 cups of mix)
6-1/2" wide X 11-1/2" high	(for 3 cups of mix)
7" wide X 13" high	(for 4 cups of mix)

Pin the two pieces of fabric together, right sides facing each other. Sew (either by hand or machine) around the sides and bottom of the bag using a 1/4" seam allowance.

To hem the top edge of the bag: Turn the top edge of the bag down 1/4" and press with an iron. Turn the pressed edge down again 1/4" and press. Stitch the hem in place close to the bottom folded edge.

Turn the bag right side out. Add the plastic bag of mix. Gather the top of the fabric bag together just above the bag of mix and tie with raffia, jute or ribbon to close.

Note: If you cut the fabric pieces using pinking shears, pin the two pieces of fabric together, wrong sides facing each other, then sew around the sides and bottom using a 1/4" seam allowance, and you won't need to turn the bag right side out or hem the top.

If you don't sew, simply bundle your plastic bag of mix inside a fabric square. Using pinking shears, cut out a square of fabric, place the bag of mix in the center, pull all four corners of the square together and tie a ribbon or jute around the gathers, close to the bag of mix. You can also use a fabric napkin or bandana (see photo on page 21).

Decorating Paper Gift Bags

Instead of a fabric gift bag, you can place your plastic bag of mix inside a paper gift bag. You can find colorful paper sacks in several sizes at craft stores or party supply stores.

If you like, you can also decorate your own sack, whether it's made from solid color paper, brown kraft paper or white paper, using some of the following suggestions:

- Use acrylic paints and stencils or rubber stamps in designs that match your gift theme, such as Christmas, Halloween, or Valentine's Day to decorate the front of your gift bag.

- Purchase colorful stickers that match your theme and adhere them to the paper bag.

- Cut a piece of printed fabric or gift wrapping paper to fit the front of your bag and adhere it using iron-on fusible web found at fabric and craft stores. Simply follow the manufacturer's instructions.

- Use colorful markers and/or glitter pens to draw a design onto your bag.

- Glue lace, paper doilies, braided trim, buttons, silk flowers or greenery or any other decorative objects that fit your gift theme onto the front.

Place a plastic bag of mix inside the paper gift sack and fold the top down about one inch. Using a standard hole punch, punch two holes about one inch apart at the center of the bag, half an inch below the fold at the top.

Thread ribbon, jute or raffia through the holes from the back to the front, and then tie the ends into a bow at the front of the sack.

Attach the cooking instruction tag to the ribbon before tying the bow.

You can also fold a paper doily in half over the top of the bag before adding the ribbon, as shown in the photo on page 57. When adding a paper doily to the top, you do not need to fold the top edge of the bag down.

Simply fold the doily in half over the top of the sack and punch two holes about one inch apart through the paper doily and sack about one half inch down from the top of the bag.

For more decoration, attach objects, such as a cinnamon stick, a wooden spoon, a tiny whisk, a cookie cutter, a candy cane, a large button, or silk flowers or greenery to the ribbon before tying into a bow at the front of the sack.

Decorating Gifts in a Jar

The ingredients that you have artfully layered into gift jars are unique and attractive, but you might want to add extra decorations to make your gift even more special.

Use your own creativity and the suggestions below to add even more color and pizzazz to your gifts.

Decorate the top of the jar with colorful print fabric. Simply cut a circle about 4 inches wider in diameter than the jar lid. It's best to use pinking shears for cutting out the fabric to prevent the fabric edges from fraying.

There are two ways to attach the circle of fabric to the jar:

Put the seal (lid) on the jar, center the fabric circle over the lid and then screw on the ring over the fabric (see the photo on page 52).

--OR--

Put the lid and ring on the jar. Center the fabric circle over the top, attach a rubber band around the ring to hold the fabric in place, then tie ribbon, raffia or jute over the rubber band and tie the ends into a bow as shown in the photograph above.

If you want the fabric to puff slightly at the top of the jar, add a small amount of polyester fiberfill stuffing on top of the lid before tying on the fabric circle.

You can also attach silk flowers, a miniature Christmas ornament, a cookie cutter, a tiny wire whisk or small wooden spoon when tying on the ribbon.

Adding Gift Tags

Don't forget to attach a gift tag to your gift that includes the name of the recipe and the instructions for preparing it. The suggestions below will give you a few ideas.

- Use a standard 3"X5" index card (white or color of your choice) or a recipe card printed with a colorful design and hand-print the instructions on it.

- You can also fold a blank 3"X5" index card in half to make a 3" wide by 2-1/2" high note card. Write the name of the recipe on the front and decorate the front with colorful stickers or markers. Print the cooking instructions on the inside of the card.

- Another option is to trace around a cookie cutter on an index card, cut out the shape, decorate it using stickers, markers, stencils, glitter or any craft medium you choose and write the recipe instructions on the back.

- If you're handy with a computer, you can design your own tag using colorful clip art or other designs, print it on card stock and cut it out. Or simply photocopy the tags in this book below each recipe, cut them out and glue them to a slightly larger piece of colored card stock using a glue stick.

- For extra decoration, cut out your tag from card stock using pinking shears or other decorative-edge scissors.

- After you have made your gift tag, use a hole punch to punch a hole at the top left corner if your tag is square or top center if your tag is round, and attach to your gift using ribbon, jute or raffia.

Gift Basket Arranging Tips

Commercial gift baskets can't compare with a personally assembled basket tailored to a friend's tastes and interests that you create for a fraction of the cost. For a little more time and a lot less money, you can assemble your own one-of-a-kind gift basket.

Attractive gift baskets are not just a matter of stuffing gift items into a container, they are carefully planned. You can create a beautiful basket with just a few gift items if you follow these steps:

1. **Pick a basket theme.** It can be a general theme such as a birthday or holiday; a product theme such as chocolate, coffee, or grilling; or a concept theme such as entertainment, sports, or house warming.

2. **Select the gift items.** Pick items that make a pleasing mix and support your theme. The size of items will help determine the shape of the finished basket. Tall items add height, medium items add bulk, and small items act as filler. Be sure to include a mix of all three to add interest and variety.

3. **Determine package style.** Place your homemade gift mixes inside attractive or unusual packaging that suits the theme. Choose eye-catching colors that coordinate with the container and paper shred. Mix or contrast textures, sizes and shapes.

4. **Pick a container.** Select a basket or container that fits the theme. Use your imagination to think of unique container ideas: a colander, a backpack, a skillet, a hat, a metal or plastic bucket, a flower pot, a mixing bowl, or a wooden crate.

5. **Coordinate the color.** Choose an overall color scheme for your basket. Color coordinate the container, gift items, ribbon, decorative embellishments and paper shred. Unfinished natural straw baskets can be spray painted to match your choice of color.

6. **Construct the Arrangement.** If your container is deep, fill the bottom with a layer of crumpled newspaper before adding your paper shred or fabric liner. Wedge heavier items, such as mugs or plates, securely down into the paper shred.

7. **Arrange the gift items.** Group the items in one of three ways: (a) Place a large item in the center, then fill in with smaller items around it. (b) Use items of similar size but varying shapes, raised at different heights to create interest. (c) Arrange an assortment of tall, medium and small gift items in descending order of height from the back of the basket to the front.

8. **Finish the arrangement.** The gift items should stand upright, not lay flat in the container. Add height to the arrangement with embellishments such as balloons, silk flowers or greenery.

You can present your gift basket unwrapped or place it in a clear acetate gift bag or wrap it in clear acetate paper. Both are sold at craft stores. Gather the top edges of the paper around the gift basket and tie on a pretty bow.

Gifts From the Heart

Experience the joy of creating your own homemade gifts, a welcome respite from today's hectic, commercially driven world that strains not only our emotions, but our budgets, as well.

Handmade gifts are much more personal than mass-produced, store-bought items because they are designed with your recipient's personal tastes and preferences in mind. You are also giving one of the most valuable gifts today—the gift of your time.

Use the tasty recipes and creative packaging ideas in this book to make hundreds of gifts for friends, co-workers and family members. Let your imagination run wild and have fun creating your own "gifts from the heart".

Index

About the Author

Gloria Hander Lyons has channeled 30 years of training and hands-on experience in the areas of art, interior decorating, crafting and event planning into writing creative how-to books. Her books cover a wide range of topics including decorating your home, cooking, planning weddings and tea parties, crafting and self-publishing.

Gloria has designed original craft projects featured in magazines, such as *Better Homes and Gardens, McCall's, Country Handcrafts* and *Crafts*.

She teaches interior decorating, event planning and self-publishing classes. Much to her family's delight, her kitchen is in non-stop test mode, creating recipes for new cookbooks.

Visit her website for free craft ideas, decorating and event planning tips and tasty recipes at:

www.BlueSagePress.com.

Other Books by Gloria Hander Lyons

- *Easy Microwave Desserts in a Mug*
- *Easy Microwave Desserts in a Mug for Kids*
- *No Rules – Just Fun Decorating*
- *Just Fun Decorating for Tweens & Teens*
- *Decorating Basics: For Men Only*
- *Ten Common Home Decorating Mistakes & How to Avoid Them*
- *If Teapots Could Talk—Fun Ideas for Tea Parties*
- *The Super-Bride's Guide for Dodging Wedding Pitfalls*
- *Lavender Sensations: Fragrant Herbs for Home & Bath*
- *A Taste of Lavender: Delectable Treats with an Exotic Floral Flavor*
- *Designs That Sell: How to Make Your Home Show Better & Sell Faster*
- *Self-Publishing on a Budget: A Do-It-All-Yourself Guide*
- *The Secret Ingredient: Tasty Recipes with an Unusual Twist*
- *Hand Over the Chocolate & No One Gets Hurt: The Chocolate-Lover's Cookbook*
- *Flamingos, Poodle Skirts & Red Hots: Creative Theme Party Ideas*

Ordering Information

To order additional copies of this book, send check or money order payable to:

 Blue Sage Press
48 Borondo Pines
La Marque, TX 77568

Cost for this edition is $6.95 per book (U.S. currency only) plus $3.00 shipping and handling for the first book and $1.50 for each additional book shipped to the same U.S. address.

Texas residents add 8.25% sales tax to total order amount.

To pay by credit card or get a complete list of books written by Gloria Hander Lyons, visit our website:

www.BlueSagePress.com

page

Made in the USA
Lexington, KY
10 September 2011